Endorsements
by Co

You are in for such a treat, as this book is life-changing. I have known Dr. Kim as a real force in the communication field and the mental health industry for over 20 years. As a clinical therapist, I have worked with hundreds of clients who supported inappropriate behaviors by remaining silent—simply dangerous! Be prepared to do some self-assessment; the only way to heal is to be real!
—DR. SABRINA JACKSON, "The People Expert" television/radio personality

"If you see something, say something" is a commonly held recommendation for those who see things or become aware of things that present a danger to personal or public safety. The term has been used by the law enforcement community to address the threat of terrorism and by school administrators and officials to address bullying. More recently, this idea of speaking up has been the voice of advocates and survivors in the #MeToo movement who have called out the perpetrators of sexual manipulation, exploitation, and abuse. At times some have shown a reluctance to raise their voices, because they feel apprehension and fear fueled by opponents who suggest such actions demonstrate disloyalty, or they believe that "snitches get stitches". The result is that they become complacent about the behaviors that they refuse to speak out against. Dr. Kim Logan-Nowlin's new book, *Cosigning Bad Behavior by Commission*

or Omission, is the psychological equivalent to the call "if you see something, say something". All of us have either witnessed or experienced the result of someone's conscientious or subconscious decisions to ignore or indulge destructive behaviors that threaten human relationships. The failure to either confront such behaviors or to actively support them is counterproductive to strong, stable families, friendships, and communities. Dr. Logan-Nowlin's almost 40 years of professional experience in the mental health arena adds integrity to her voice as she provides a process for determining when a person is cosigning bad behavior. Her counsel highlights the best ways to respond, so that individuals can foster positive, productive relationships.
—KENNETH ANDERSON, M.S., executive director,
Leadership Empowerment Enterprise

The book *Cosigning Bad Behavior by Commission or Omission* is one of the most powerful and informative books I have read in this decade. This book is needed in a generation where inhumane and unchecked behaviors are endorsed by commission and omission especially if fame or fortune are at stake. Dr. Kim points out that detrimental actions may occur if there is fear of the loss of a relationship, or when a cosigner to the bad behavior does not see the need to stand up for those who can't stand up for themselves. She shows us in this book that cosigning bad behavior leaves a person in a state of internal confusion, depression, and loneliness, and that it affects the person who performs the bad behavior as well as the cosigner. The author has called each of us to stop cosigning bad behavior. Dr. Kim's professional

training and keen insight on the subject matter makes her a perfect writer and practitioner to open up a new understanding of what bad behavior is, how we contribute by commission or omission, and how it can be stopped. If you love a good read, are a caring and open-minded person, and are ready to be "woke" about the subject of *Cosigning Bad Behavior by Commission or Omission*, this is definitely the book for you! I dare say that this book should be a New York Times Best Seller. Thank you, Dr. Kim, for this book. It will be of good use to many today, tomorrow, and in the years to come.
—DR. JANICE JOHNSON BROWNE, Ph.D., GCM, chaplain, educator, author, life coach, leadership consultant, suicide prevention specialist, and international inspirational speaker

I am so honored to support Dr. Kim Logan-Nowlin on her journey to create awareness and stand up to bad behaviors which are often ignored. I met Dr. Kim approximately ten years ago, and it has been a joy to see how she and her late husband Arthur E. Nowlin, LMSW, counseled, mentored, and partnered to write various books that shed light on important issues. They have worked tirelessly to help our communities to be mentally, emotionally, and spiritually healthy. I am beyond disappointed by the way society, in many cases, chooses to ignore bad behavior based on who is involved. Whether we live in the best suites or the worst streets, we should not cosign bad behavior! It is disgusting to turn on the news at any given time and witness unacceptable behavior in the White House, school houses, church houses, and in our neighborhoods. As a chaplain, I often see

situations that could have been prevented, but someone did nothing because they got a payoff, it wasn't their child, or the victim was not from their community, ethnic group, or social economic status. We have a long way to go, and now is the time to stop cosigning bad behavior on all levels!
—Dr. PORTIA LOCKETT, chaplain

Cosigning Bad Behavior by Commission or Omission is a wakeup call for any parent, educator, or childcare provider. We recognize that children have various needs, concerns, and fears, and that they need loving support and guidance. However, as adults, when it comes to doing what is right for them and on their behalf, we often lack the integrity and skills to do so. It is critical for individuals and organizations, responsible for their well-being, to stop ignoring issues that lead to negative outcomes and consequences which are affecting children's lives. Take a stand! Knowing when and how to speak up and speak out, to protect young lives and future generations, may not always be easy; but it is necessary if we desire to exhibit the love of God and protect our most precious possessions—our children. Standing up for our youth not only takes courage, but also guidance and support from others to help address difficult circumstances. *Cosigning Bad Behavior by Commission or Omission* provides readers with the tools and inspiration to raise up and educate children and youth in healthy and caring environments.
—RENEE LOGAN HUMPHREYS, M.A., M.Ed., parent, teacher, and education administrator

COSIGNING
BAD BEHAVIOR
By Commission or Omission

COSIGNING
BAD BEHAVIOR
By Commission or Omission

KIM LOGAN-NOWLIN, PH.D., LPC

Foreword by
PASTOR AUSTIN HUMPHREYS, M.A.

XULON PRESS

Xulon Press
2301 Lucien Way #415
Maitland, FL 32751
407.339.4217
www.xulonpress.com

© 2020 by Kim Logan- Nowlin, Ph.D., LPC
Revised 2021

Cosigning Bad Behavior by Commission or Omission
by Kim Logan-Nowlin, Ph.D., LPC

Senior Editor: Debbie Battin Sasser, M.A.
Book Cover: Albert Rodgers, Ennis Woods
Contributing Writers: Arthur Nowlin, LMSW; Pastor Austin Humphreys, M.A.; and Ennis Woods

All rights reserved solely by the author. The author guarantees all contents are original and do not infringe upon the legal rights of any other person or work. No part of this book may be reproduced in any form without the permission of the author. The views expressed in this book are not necessarily those of the publisher.

Unless otherwise indicated, Scripture quotations taken from the King James Version (KJV)—*public domain*. Scripture quotations also taken from the Holy Bible, New International Version (NIV). Copyright © 1973, 1978, 1984, 2011 by Biblica, Inc.™. Used by permission. All rights reserved.

Printed in the United States of America.

ISBN-13: 978-1-6305-0454-0
Ebook: 978-1-6305-0455-7

For information:
Kim Logan-Nowlin Communications, Inc.
3011 W. Grand Blvd. Suite 423
Detroit, Michigan 48202
www.drkiminspires.com
www.xulonpress.com

Presented to

_____

By

_____

Special Occasion

_____

Date

_____

"Don't pick up the pen!"

I give honor to God for giving me the opportunity to share this book with you. I am blessed and grateful to God for giving me the vision, desire, and patience to not give up on this long and difficult journey. I write this book in love and in memory of my late husband, Arthur E. Nowlin, LMSW, FMSW, CAADC, AAFLP.

—Dr. Kim Logan-Nowlin, Ph.D.

Dedication

This book is dedicated to individuals in relationships at home, at work, and in the community, who stand up for what is right, who speak out against what is wrong, and who do not support or lend a hand by cosigning bad behavior. To God be the glory!

"I am what I cosign."
Dr. Kim Logan-Nowlin

*"Leaders are not above the law
and are not above God's Holy Word."*
Dr. Kim Logan-Nowlin

"In the end, we will remember not the words of our enemies, but the silence of our friends."
Dr. Martin Luther King, Jr.

A Legacy of Love

In Loving Memory
of
Arthur E. Nowlin, LMSW
July 3, 1948 – October 28, 2016

As this book was in the initial stages, my children, family, friends, and I, were deeply saddened by the unexpected loss of my dear, loving husband and partner in the Lord. Arthur passed away on October 28, 2016. From the moment I met my amazing Arthur, he was always excited about life, learning, sharing information, and helping to improve the quality of life in others. Arthur, until the moment of his last breath, loved and served the Lord with gladness and faithfulness. His favorite song: "I Am Not Ashamed" truly gave meaning and purpose to his life. He treasured and loved his three children: Jason, Micha, and Erin, and his grandson Phoenix.

This book is dedicated to the loving memory and legacy of Arthur E. Nowlin, LMSW, FMSW, CAADC, AAFLP —man of God, husband, father, social worker, advocate, author, speaker, veteran, golfer, television host, and visionary.

*"Become your own change agent,
and do not cosign bad behavior."*
Arthur E. Nowlin

Table of Contents

Dedication xv
A Legacy of Love xxi
Foreword xxv
Preface. xxvii
Introduction xxxi

Chapter One —
   What is Cosigning Bad Behavior? 1

Chapter Two —
   What are the Causes of Cosigning Bad Behavior? 9

Chapter Three —
   When Do I Stop Being an Enabler? 21

Chapter Four —
   Discouraging Bad Behavior: No More Passes 29

Chapter Five —
   Train Up a Child. 35

Chapter Six —
   What Does It Profit a Man to Gain Then Lose? 41

Chapter Seven —
  Inner Peace is Priceless 47

Chapter Eight —
  Committed to Integrity........................... 55

Chapter Nine —
  Standing on Honesty 63

Chapter Ten —
  Blackmailed to Cosign 69

Chapter Eleven —
  No More Secrets................................. 75

Chapter Twelve —
  ". . . Even in the Church!" 89

Chapter Thirteen —
  Vision of Excellence 97

Bad Behavior Contract 106
Bibliography 111
Reader Reflections................................ 113
Author's Bio..................................... 119
Other Featured Books 123
Book Dr. Kim for Your Next Event 133
About Kim Logan-Nowlin Communications Clinic, Inc . 137

Foreword

I started my ministry as an associate pastor in Atlanta, Georgia, where I ministered to over 1,300 people on a weekly basis. My tenure there taught me several lessons to strengthen my ministry, but none more important than the art of dealing with people. A successful pastor understands the importance of managing situations that can stem from negative and toxic behavior. Now years later, as the senior pastor of two churches, those lessons on managing all types of behavior are key to the success of my ministry. Many know the author of this book as Dr. Kim Logan-Nowlin, I've always known her as Auntie Kim. As a natural-born advocate, she willingly engages the threat of conflict in order to promote a positive outcome.

Dr. Kim Logan-Nowlin's new book, *Cosigning Bad Behavior by Commission or Omission*, calls for a mature level of transparency in relationships which does away with the mindset—"don't ask, don't tell". For so long, many individuals have lived with toxic relationships that embrace the mindset of "sweep it under the rug" or "this is just who they are" excuses. Failure to speak up against serious issues causes many to live in unproductive, dysfunctional, and toxic relationships.

All of us, one way or another, have seen and encountered people who indulge in toxic behavior. Whether they are friends, coworkers, family members, or significant others, we have a responsibility to speak out against things that negatively impact our relationships. Failure to do so supports and encourages counterproductive behavior. Dr. Logan-Nowlin, with her decades of experience in the areas of mental health and psychology, provides productive insight on how to positively address damaging issues. Her book is designed to help individuals recognize and dismantle toxic behavior while providing the reader with the tools to address and maintain progressive, healthy relationships. Dr. Logan-Nowlin inspires people to speak out against the wrongs they see and to embrace a constructive culture.

—Pastor Austin Humphreys, M.A.

PREFACE

"Commitment to Change"

Cosigning Bad Behavior by Commission or Omission is revolutionary in nature, and provides foundational principles and praxis that will inspire us to recover and strengthen families, churches, and communities. I believe this book is groundbreaking in that it causes us to confront issues that are so often, to our own detriment, swept under the carpet. How often do we in the church cosign bad behavior because we were too scared, too lazy, or too greedy to speak up? As a church leader, I am keenly aware of numerous situations where the church has cosigned bad behavior by commission or omission; because we didn't want to lose personal friendships, titles, positions, or because we felt it was not our business.

Dr. Martin Luther King, Jr. said, "He who passively accepts evil is as much involved in it as he who helps to perpetrate it. He who accepts evil without protesting against it is really cooperating with it." From the very beginning of time, the Bible tells us that Adam cosigned the imperfect behavior of his wife Eve in disobeying God by eating from the tree of the knowledge of good and evil. In 1 Samuel 2, Priest Eli cosigned the negative behaviors of his sons by allowing their actions and by his failure to speak out against their conduct. If King David had not been sternly counseled by the prophet Nathan he may have continued in his wicked behavior (2 Samuel 12).

Cosigning Bad Behavior by Commission or Omission provides readers with the tools needed to create change and recover a generation of people who have been taught to keep silent. This book is a must-read for all church leaders, administrators, and laity so that we can live healthy, authentic, Christ-centered lives free of guilt and shame.

—William Jeffery Lee, Sr., D. Min., is a pastor and the men's ministries leader in the Lake Region Conference of Seventh-day Adventists, author of *Ready, Set, Go! Igniting African American Men for Christ,* television host of "For Guys Only" on the Dare to Dream Network, a parent, and an international speaker.

"Bad behavior becomes worse once you cosign it."
Dr. Kim Logan-Nowlin

Introduction

Cosigning bad behavior is a silent, destructive act that can tear apart the fragments of a relationship, a healthy family structure, one's reputation, or a cooperative business partnership. Cosigning bad behavior can cloud the lens of politics and destroy the foundation of a church. As a community we have a responsibility to stand up for what is right, and warn others that a negative lifestyle of dishonesty will not be tolerated within our relationships.

I hope that this book will empower and inspire others to not support or cosign bad behavior in any circumstance. You have the choice to pick up the pen or not when it comes to cosigning bad behavior. What will it be? Misery loves company—it does not need your help or permission, and it certainly

Cosigning Bad Behavior by Commission or Omission

does not need your signature. Don't pick up the pen and cosign negative behavior.

Many relationships are destroyed and hardships created as a result of people making conscious decisions to cosign someone's bad behavior. Harmful behaviors often get longevity because people choose to remain silent. They observe and recognize what is happening in the situation but won't do anything to prevent or discourage the act. Cosigning is sometimes an excuse used to support a friend or to safeguard the cosigner's anonymity against unexpected failure. Many times, people support the cosigning of bad behavior because they somewhat agree with what the other person is doing or the expected end result. In other words, "I know what you are doing is wrong, but I will benefit from the act, so therefore I won't say anything."

This book has been written to encourage you to think twice before you, knowingly or unintentionally, support something that you don't agree with, believe in, or wouldn't do yourself. The biggest life-support connected to bad behavior is the way that people choose not to speak out against it. Cosigning is not always a bad thing, and it can demonstrate love and support for others around us. It has been a tool used to help a grassroots business to blossom into a successful business, to help a student finance their education, to acquire a car loan, or to give a name to be used as a reference.

However, this book addresses the cosigning of bad behavior. By not speaking out against what is wrong, you may be cosigning destructive behavior. Many cosigners will choose to remain silent because they are afraid to say something or are benefiting

Introduction

from the act. The overall importance of my desire in sharing this book with you is to help you, the reader, to remain focused on your vision. Our silence or refusal to get involved is giving longevity and life to bad behavior. For the sake of our own well-being and for the good of all those we encounter on a daily basis, we should never cosign bad behavior.

—Kim Logan-Nowlin, Ph.D.

"If you lack wisdom, ask God."
James 1:5

Chapter 1

What is Cosigning Bad Behavior?

Cosigning: The act of signing cooperatively with someone.
Bad behavior: A negative way a person acts or demonstrates harmful conduct.
Commission: The act of carrying out or perpetrating something (a mistake, crime, or immoral act).
Omission: The act of failing to do something, especially something that a person has a moral or legal obligation to do.

Is it wrong to recognize bad behavior and then cosign it? Yes, it is! As a specialist in the mental health profession for over 37 years, one of my greatest concerns is to help eliminate negative behavior by utilizing different therapeutic processes.

Recognizing, cosigning, and remaining silent doesn't assist in teaching others to be accountable for their behaviors. If there isn't any accountability, it is the same as being complacent. To be silent can give a false sense of approval or send an erroneous message that a person's bad behavior does not have any negative consequences.

The primary concern is how to address the matter, especially if it is a sensitive situation. Most importantly, you don't want to give the impression that you support the negative behavior by laughing, remaining silent about the issue, or making gestures that suggest the behavior is acceptable. These reactions give the appearance that you are supporting the negative behaviors. Sometimes when people are committing bad behavior, they will look at you for a response. If you are not direct in your objection to what they are doing or may do, the person is likely to interpret this as silent support and they will think that you are condoning their behavior. Examples of this type of situation could be: a medical staff member knowing that the doctors are writing fake or inappropriate prescriptions, teachers passing underachieving students to make themselves look successful, a repair person doing unnecessary repairs or no repairs at all but still charging the customer, an employee falsifying time sheets for payroll purposes, and political figures using tax dollars for personal use. These are behaviors that need to be addressed.

I am not going to be dishonest, cheat, embarrass myself, or bring shame to my family or coworkers just to be accepted or viewed as successful. Having integrity is an important factor in my work as a therapist. My clients must be able to trust me and see that I am transparent, and therefore, I can freely suggest what is best for them to do to achieve a positive outcome.

There are many challenges that we face throughout our lifetime. Yet, these challenges can offer tremendous opportunities if we make the right choices. How many times are we faced with decisions and the fear of failure? At those times, it is important to look at our opportunities as motivation for success and to not allow ourselves to cosign negative behavior. When we are not connected to a support system, this void causes us to battle within ourselves to make positive changes.

Our relationships with our loved ones should be important enough to us that we strive to improve our overall attitude and exhibit compassion. If we are not implementing patience, understanding, and love, it becomes paramount to discover what is necessary to improve our relationships. Taking the first step towards healing should not be a barrier causing extended anguish in the relationship. Here are some basic therapeutic tools to eliminate cosigning bad behavior in your relationships:

1. Admit that there is something wrong or that a bad behavior is taking place.
2. Establish positive dialogue to correct the wrong by recognizing and acknowledging the negative behavior.
3. Learn how to address, confront, and separate yourself from any negativity involved.

These basic tips are the starting point that allows the first step of healing. We can never stop improving who we are, and we must understand how important it is to maintain a positive environment for our families and loved ones. We must take the necessary risk to improve our lives and stop cosigning negative behavior.

"When you see something, know better, and you don't do anything about it, you have cosigned that bad behavior."
Dr. Kim Logan-Nowlin

Case Study: "Just One Thank You"

Wynter Edwards is in her freshman year of college. She is your typical college student and enjoys the college life of friendships, student-style fashions, and socializing. She loves dressing nice, the attention she receives, and has never met a camera that she didn't love. Wynter spends quite a bit of her extra money from her parents and from her campus job to buy the latest designer clothes and accessories. One day Wynter's mother, Mrs. Edwards, was in the store shopping when a new line of designer clothing was being released. She thought, "What great timing! Wynter will love these new fashions!" Knowing her sizes, her mother picked out five complete outfits for her daughter. After much thought, Mrs. Edwards bought the items and immediately took them to the post office for next day delivery.

Mrs. Edwards knew that her daughter would be ecstatic about the clothing, which was scheduled to be delivered by noon the next day. Later the next day, Mrs. Edwards wondered why she had not received a phone call acknowledging the fact that her daughter had received the shipment, especially considering that Wynter had already posted pictures on social media of herself wearing the new outfits. Mrs. Edwards just wrote it off as excitement, and imagined that she had simply forgotten to call her mother to thank her.

Wynter was very accustomed to receiving unexpected packages and gifts from her mother. Several days passed and after a few more gifts were sent to her, again there was no response. Wynter's mom began to realize that her kindness and thoughtfulness appeared to be unappreciated and was being taken for granted. This bothered her so much that she called her daughter and said, "Wynter, do you have something to say to me?" Wynter's response was, "Hi Mom! What are you talking about?" Mrs. Edwards explained to her daughter that she had been raised to show appreciation and be thankful for all acts of kindness, especially unsolicited generosity, no matter how big or small. She repeated her favorite quote to her daughter, "People don't have to be nice to you, not even your parents." Wynter was somewhat stunned, and responded, "Okay Mom . . . where is this coming from?" Mrs. Edwards said, "Never mind. Have a good evening," and immediately hung up the telephone.

After ending the conversation, Mrs. Edward did a self-assessment and reflected about what had happened to her daughter's disposition. She realized that she had not identified nor corrected Wynter's ungrateful behavior in previous situations for fear that her daughter would reject her. This oversight of the problem had continued, and had now become normal behavior for Wynter. Mrs. Edwards had never addressed the problem when it first appeared many months ago, but had chosen to remain silent. Therefore, Mrs. Edwards was guilty of cosigning bad behavior by omission.

"It is said that silence is golden, but it can also be destructive."
Dr. Kim Logan-Nowlin

Chapter 2

What Are the Causes of Cosigning Bad Behavior?

One important major cause for cosigning bad behavior is fear. Fear is something that manifests itself within our character. It creates barriers to achieving our personal goals and objectives. We need to recognize that fear exists. Also, we need to understand the tools needed to reconstruct our approach to fear in a healthy manner. Fear impacts our lives in every aspect. If we are unable to address the barrier of fear in a positive way, it will be a destructive force throughout our lifetime.

How can we better understand fear as it relates to cosigning bad behavior? When individuals cosign, out of fear, they are saying, "I want to be accepted, I don't want to be disliked. I want to be loved, I don't want to be the one to disrupt the plan or action. I want to be valued, and I want to feel like I am your equal." Fear will cause you to lie, cover up the truth, alienate your family, and present a false image of yourself.

Fear also will cause you to believe that you are the most important person in a negative situation. For example, when a criminal act is being performed by a person in a position of power or fame, they use that same power to brain wash, manipulate, or control the mind of another human being. People must learn how to say: "No, I can't, I won't, and I'm not going to support this action by cosigning your bad behavior." People need to think about the worst possible outcome or what the effects will be of the decision that they are contemplating before picking up the pen to cosign the behavior.

Studies have shown that unless past negative experiences have been addressed through professional help, these behaviors can carry over far into a person's adult life. Aggressive behavior is an associated symptom of many psychiatric disorders and can manifest itself throughout a person's life span—from Attention-Deficit Hyperactivity Disorder (ADHD) in children and adolescents, to domestic violence or dementia in adults. While much of the literature on aggression has focused on adolescents and adults, less attention has been given to understanding the etiology of aggressive behaviors across the entire developmental spectrum. Listed below are some red flag behaviors that may indicate that you or someone you know are practicing bad behavior.

What Are the Causes of Cosigning Bad Behavior?

Dishonesty
Fear
Revenge
Personal gain
Guilt
Lying
Stress
Impulsive/Lack of self-control
Desperation
Illegal acts
Manipulation
Blackmail/Coercion/Extortion
Intimidation/Bullying
Abuse
Disrespect/Rudeness
Accepting payoffs/bribes
Stealing
Profanity
Falsifying documents and records

These types of bad behaviors, when not professionally and therapeutically addressed, manifest in repeat patterns. Change is possible through the use of what is called the Transtheoretical Model, which was developed by professor James O. Prochaska of the University of Rhode Island, Carlo Di Clemente, and their colleagues. This Model is helpful in discovering why individuals behave the way they do, and includes the following stages: precontemplation, contemplation, preparation for action, action, and maintenance. People may oscillate back and forth between the various steps for many months or years before achieving long-lasting change in their behaviors. This model is frequently used by experts when counseling clients with alcohol or drug addiction problems. Let's explore these stages in more detail:

1. **Precontemplation**

In this stage, individuals are not aware that they have a problem and are actively engaging in risky behaviors such as excessive smoking, drinking, using drugs, gambling, engaging in unsafe sexual practices, or lying. It's important to keep in mind that people are engaging in these risky behaviors for a reason.

Whether a person is drinking to numb the grief of a broken marriage, or snorting cocaine to get high and be accepted by their friends, these behaviors all have one thing in common— they work. In the short-term, these behaviors provide immediate relief from stress, and make you feel good, accepted, and as though your life is problem-free. In the long term, they can have devastating consequences, ruin lives, and can even be fatal.

2. **Contemplation**

In this stage, the thought may occur to an individual that they actually have a problem. Friends, relatives, or other community members may be commenting on their substance use or behavior. They may be arrested for driving under the influence or end up in the emergency department with an accidental, recreational drug overdose. A physician may point out that their abnormal blood work results are indicative of liver damage due to excessive alcohol consumption. This is when their behaviors are resulting in unexpected consequences such as others taking notice, health problems, or intervention by authorities.

3. **Preparation for Action**

In this stage, the individual acknowledges and accepts the fact that their behavior is problematic, and they are considering what to do. Family and friends can provide assistance by encouraging the individual to seek professional help. Now is the time when the individual can benefit from information on treatment options including the names, phone numbers, and contact information for treatment centers, their local Alcohol Anonymous (AA) chapter, or mental health and addictions counselors. When people with addiction problems contact the emergency department due to adverse health symptoms related to their addiction, they are provided with pamphlets or phone numbers of treatment agencies. In order for change to be effective, however, they must be the one, not hospital staff, to make the phone call to the treatment agencies.

4. **Action**

In this stage, the individual takes action. Action can be seen in various forms including calling the treatment agency, attending AA meetings, scheduling an appointment with a doctor, going for counselling, or quitting cold turkey. Alcoholics or drug addicts who suddenly stop using the substance can develop a dangerous condition known as delirium tremens, which if left untreated can prove fatal. An alcoholic or drug addict may need to check-in and stay at an in-house detox facility or treatment center for an extended period of time. Treatment may also be forced upon an individual by the court system due to criminal behaviors stemming from their addictions.

It can be helpful for people to change certain elements in their environment to foster success. This may include disposing of any cigarettes, drugs, or alcohol that they may possess, or even moving to a new neighborhood and cutting ties with their substance-abusing friends. These changes are recommended because "misery loves company", and people who are using will try to pull their recovering friends back down.

At this stage individuals may not be fully prepared to commit. They may still be waffling back and forth. For example, they may call addictions services but fail to follow through with their appointments. For those who do follow through on all of the necessary actions, they move on to the final stage of change, maintenance.

5. **Maintenance**

During this stage, an individual has successfully changed their behavior and is reaping the rewards. They may be attending AA meetings regularly, going to counselling, or simply no longer doing the counterproductive behaviors. However, if confronted by serious life stressors such as the death of a loved one, divorce, or illness, they may be vulnerable to "falling off the wagon" and ending up right back where they started from—at the precontemplation stage. Some recovering alcoholics and drug addicts will find themselves moving through these stages multiple times before achieving long-term success. It is, therefore, helpful to know which stage an individual is in so that the appropriate interventions can be enacted. Dependencies and addictions of any type are detrimental to anyone's health and mental abilities. The last thing that an individual with this problem needs is a friend or family member who supports, ignores, or cosigns the bad behavior.

"The act of endurance initiates the challenge of triumph."
Arthur & Kim Nowlin

Case Study: "Willing to Cheat for Gain"

Mike has been using his accountant, Henry, for many years to file his taxes. Over the years he did not have any complaints with Henry's work. Each year, Mike would receive a large tax refund which would help him with his bills and other expenses. After giving his tax and payroll information to Henry, he informed Mike that if he reported the last $5,000 that he had earned in December, it would put him in an entirely different tax bracket. Henry then replied, "Listen, I can save you a few thousand dollars by just omitting the December earnings with one easy click of my computer mouse. What do you want me to do? I know what I would do if it were me?" Mike happily said, "You're the accountant, go for it! The savings will help me pay for my annual cruise this summer."

Mike recognized his dishonesty which is one the characteristics of bad behavior. He approved and supported the decision by authorizing his accountant Henry to cheat and lie on his tax records for financial gain. This dishonest act could have caused Henry to lose his Certified Public Accounting (CPA) license. Mike was not concerned about the consequences of Henry's act. All he could see was the financial reward. Henry was a cheater, and when Mike cosigned the behavior, he became a coconspirator and cheater also. Through direct deposit Mike received his tax refund of $17,000, and he happily tipped Henry $2,000, and said, "Thanks for looking out." Although Mike received a large refund, his situation was not over yet. The IRS conducted an audit, found the error, and filed charges against Henry and

Mike for their dishonesty. Henry lost his license as a CPA, and Mike had to pay a large fine.

"Sometimes, it's not what you do, but what you don't do that has the greatest impact and influence."
Dr. Kim Logan-Nowlin

Chapter 3

When Do I Stop Being An Enabler?

Enable: The authority or means to do something, or encouraging self-destructive behavior.

Enabler: A person who encourages or enables negative or self-destructive behavior in another person.

When a person chooses to engage in impulsive or self-destructive behavior, it is advisable to assess the problem which is enticing the negative behavior. Unfortunately, the person, who may have good intentions to stop the behavior from occurring, sometimes becomes an active player in the situation by endorsing the behavior. An enabler is someone who fixes, ignores, or covers-up someone else's dangerous mistakes or actions, preventing the other person from receiving the consequences or being held accountable. It is important to develop healthy boundaries to prevent a family member or friend from continuing to do at-risk behaviors, otherwise there could be serious consequences for all parties involved.

Often times, when bad behavior gets out of control it can become breaking, headline news. Reports that spread about criminal acts or other negative actions can be something as minor as water cooler chatter or as serious as a life-altering situation. People, who have cosigned bad behavior, begin to feel guilty, because they realize that it wasn't just about their own selfishness, greed, fear, or interest in the situation. They begin to see that there are actual victims involved who have suffered, possibly unnecessarily, and their lives have been altered or affected in negative ways, too. People familiar with a situation usually come to believe later that, just maybe, if they had only spoken up to discourage the behavior, it could have possibly been prevented. These people are defined as enablers whether their actions were intentional or unintentional.

There are actions that can be taken to prevent yourself or others from becoming enablers. When you recognize the behavior, speak out boldly and truthfully against it. Explain the possible outcomes and consequences, and realize that someone may be a victim as a result of this behavior, and that it can have a domino effect, devastating many lives, sprouting in many directions. A person should not be a cosigner for an enabler.

Neither should a person want their name, reputation, or their work damaged or scandalized by being associated or involved in bad behaviors.

My late husband, Arthur E. Nowlin, committed his life to helping people to release themselves from being a hostage of drug addiction. In his seminars and training, he constantly emphasized "instant gratification". There is a common phrase that says, "I want what I want when I want it". This is a very dangerous concept or way of life for enablers, because they don't think about the awful consequences that they are allowing themselves to be a part of, nor are they taking the time to process their choices. Making a conscientious decision leads to healthier and more positive outcomes within situations.

According to Summer Jeirles, a Licensed Professional Counselor, in an article on the American Counseling Association website, the last form of enabling, as a result of denial, is the thought process that denies the fact that the family member or friend has become an alcoholic/addict because _____(insert a preconceived idea). The parent or loved one injects their own views of addiction, and comes to the conclusion that their loved one can't possibly be an addict, because he or she: has a good job, has a degree, comes from a good home, only drinks or uses drugs on weekends or after work, doesn't use drugs/drink all day, they don't drink/use drugs as much as so and so—or fill in the blank with whatever else you want. These, interestingly, are the same thought patterns that show up in the person who has the active addiction, "I can't be an addict/alcoholic because _____."

When families or friends reinforce this thought pattern, it only fuels the destructive behavior and keeps the person in active addiction.

The bottom line is that when someone is an active addict, the person's loved ones can go through different versions of denial which can lead to enabling. Some questions that pop up for them are:

What does it say about me if my son/daughter/husband/wife is an alcoholic/drug addict?

What will I have to do if they are?

What will I tell the rest of the family?

What will I tell our friends?

What will they think of us?

What if he/she never wants to get help? What will I need to do then?

These questions, as well as many others are an enabler's excuses. The answers to these questions can be too painful for someone to face, and, as a result, they may believe that it is easier to live in denial and continue to enable.

"Think about the worst consequence that can result from the decision that you are about to make?"
Dr. Kim Logan-Nowlin

Case Study: "The Cover Up of an Emotional Affair"

Phillip and Sarah have been happily married for ten years. The couple worked at the post office, and both shared a common friend named Eddie. Eddie always admired Phillip and Sarah's relationship. One day Phillip talked with Eddie about some marital problems that he and Sarah had been having for quite a while. Phillip found comfort in another coworker named Sheila. Talking to her and getting a female perspective and advice on how to handle his martial situation was comforting to him. Phillip would tell Eddie that Sheila was a great listener and that is what he felt was missing in his marriage with Sarah.

Phillip was slowly developing an emotional affair with Sheila. They were sharing lunch together and often assisting one another at work. Eddie knew about the relationship but didn't say anything. One day Phillip asked Eddie to cover for him if his wife were to call and ask for him. He wanted Eddie to lie and say that he was out taking care of an emergency job assignment that had come up. Eddie was puzzled and wanted to know why? Phillip told him, while winking, that he and Sarah were meeting at an establishment downtown for a couple of hours for drinks and so-called "shop talk".

One hour later Sarah called Eddie and asked if Phillip was there, because she was expecting him to be home already, and she had not heard from him. Eddie told Sarah that Phillip was on an important work assignment offsite, and he would be finished in about two hours. Sarah wondered why Phillip didn't bother to just call and tell her. Eddie lied again and said, "The station has poor phone reception." Sarah felt at ease and said, "I'll see him when he gets home." Eddie felt guilty for lying to Sarah and covering up for his friend.

Eddie enabled and cosigned Phillip's unfaithfulness and bad behavior. Eddie should have told Phillip that he was not going to lie. He could have discussed the possible damage that his actions could do to his marriage and advise him to not go through with the clandestine meeting. Phillip may have changed his mind. Eddie was not being a true friend. He was a cosigning enabler.

"Your signature exposes your character."
Dr. Kim Logan-Nowlin

Chapter 4

Discouraging Bad Behavior: No More Passes

Discourage: To prevent or seek to prevent something by showing disapproval or creating intentional obstacles.

It is important to recognize what bad behavior is and what makes it unacceptable. Often people become exposed to various opportunities that can cause a person to indulge in negative behavior that will most likely produce a negative outcome. The outcomes could very well cost an individual their freedom or even their life. We must not be afraid to address the problems, the causes, and the consequences of bad behavior.

During counseling, the patient is provided treatment with the singular goal that healing will occur. If the individual that is administering treatment is not being successful, then another alternative to treatment must be available. The paradigm shift theory, as identified by philosopher Thomas Kuhn, is a change from one way of thinking to another. A paradigm shift will force the person being treated to try another strategy to discourage the bad behavior, after other attempts and methods have not worked. The paradigm shift shines new light on the situation, which will lead the process potentially outside of the usual and accepted way of doing something or thinking about it.

A major concern when you are discussing change is the need to determine whether the new methods implemented are being successful or falling short of the goal. It is not easy to define success or failure, because change can be subtle and abstract. The paradigm shift can occur through the implementation of various strategies, always with the end goal of healing and recovery. These are some counseling steps to help those who are aware of their need to change, and who no longer want free passes for bad behavior:

1. Admit that there is a problem.
2. Take action to solve the problem.
3. Visualize yourself changing.
4. Implement a daily, personal inventory of your decision-making processes.
5. Be proactive about your outcomes.
6. Pray for spiritual guidance.
7. Seek godly counseling.

"A person should not be a cosigner for an enabler."
Dr. Kim Logan-Nowlin

Case Study: "Caught in The Act"

Martha is a single mother with four children. She was employed as a teller at a local bank for the past ten years in the downtown area. As a teller, she served an average of about 150 customers per day collecting and processing thousands and thousands of dollars each day. She laughed and joked with her co-workers, saying, "I have $2 in my pocket, and I have $2,000 that pass through my fingers into this cash drawer." Despite her full-time job and salary, she struggled to make ends meet, living pay check to pay check. Often, her bills came before her payday. To prevent any shut off notices or emergencies that might arise unexpectedly, Martha took money out of her drawer on Thursday and replaced it on her payday the following Friday.

Her coworker Terri and some of the other tellers knew that she was taking and replacing money for several weeks. There were other tellers, with the exception of Terri, who were doing the same thing. Terri talked to Martha on many different occasions about how she could lose her job if her actions were discovered. Martha tried to explain to Terri about all the pressure that she was under just to survive.

Terri told Martha that her financial struggles do not justify her stealing from the bank. The bad behavior did not stop, until Terri explained the full consequences of stealing and that Martha could be suspended, terminated, and face federal criminal charges if caught, charged, and convicted. She also told her that she could be separated from her children for many years if she received a prison sentence. From that moment forward, Martha never took any more money from her cash drawer. She was thankful that her coworker helped her see the light, reminded her of the big picture, and helped prevent her from the traumatic experience of losing her job or her freedom. Terri refused to cosign Martha's bad behavior.

Life-sustaining support is given to bad behavior many times by those who are close to you, mainly from enabling family members, co-workers, and close friends. Because of the close relationships, bad behaviors are often ignored or joked about. They are called "free passes" to bad behavior. These "free passes" can be more harmful than the erroneous actions of cosigners who don't know you personally. The family members, co-workers, and close friends should be familiar with your faults, weaknesses, and short comings. They should know better and should not hesitate to correct you when you are on a downward, destructive path. The expectation should be that loved ones are the last people who should ever give out "free passes" for bad behavior. Under no circumstances and at no time should bad behavior be ignored. With the right support, these negative behaviors can be changed into positive outcomes.

"Train up a child in the way he should go: and when he is old, he will not depart from it."
Proverbs 22:6

Chapter 5

Train Up a Child...

The mind of a child and his or her habits are formed at an early age. Statistically, early childhood, which spans up to eight years of age, is a critical time for cognitive, social, emotional, and physical development. During this time span, children are responsive to change. The behaviors that you allow or teach during their childhood, whether they are positive or negative behaviors, have a tremendous influence on their lives.

At this early age, a child should be in a positive learning environment, around positive people, while allowed to still be a child. Appropriate, timely discipline should not be withheld while training the child to learn and conduct themselves according to their age and developmental level. When a child's negative behavior is ignored, it is mostly visible in a public setting or around other children. To ignore this behavior is cosigning childhood problems. This is a sure avenue to having a child with behavior problems that continue as they grow.

As a parent, you should develop coping strategies that work for you and your child. Try to implement techniques that reinforce positive development and character-building. It is important to identify the psychological needs of your child in order to address their negative behavior. As you plan daily for new social development and positive interaction, your child will develop stronger control over his or her emotions and gain the ability to moderate their negative moods.

When identifying your child's needs you want to take a personal inventory of their personal and physical well-being. It is imperative that parents learn effective tools to help recognize trauma in a child's life and to identify any unusual change in their behavior. When a child's development is interrupted by a negative situation, more than likely the child will respond in a way that could cause him/her to mask their pain. It is imperative that parents and guardians seek help when their child has unexplained changes in their behavior which could indicate that they have experienced something traumatic. Trained psychologists, therapists, and counselors are a source for parents in need of help navigating behavior problems or sensitive issues in their children's lives.

"You have a valid reason to believe that I am what I cosign."
Dr. Kim Logan-Nowlin

Case Study: "No Justification"

Anita was 27 years old and a stay-at-home mother. She maintained her home while her husband worked day shifts at his job. She had three small children ages three, four, and six. After Anita finished her household chores, she gathered the children together and took them to the supermarket. The children were healthy and energetic and looked forward to going on their weekly outing to the store. When Anita entered the store, she put the youngest child in the cart, and the two older children walked beside her.

The store was crowded, and the children were excited about seeing all of the people and all of the goodies and snacks throughout the store. This setting made the children very playful and lively. Her youngest child, who was riding in the basket, was rocking back and forth, causing her mother to have difficulty with controlling the shopping cart, often bumping into product displays and customers. The other two children went running down the aisle pulling toys and snacks off of the shelves, while screaming as though they were on the playground. The screaming alarmed the customers in the store and they thought the children had been hurt. When one customer mentioned to Anita that the children were being rowdy and might hurt themselves. Anita replied, "Oh it's alright. They are just children, and I have an eye on them."

Anita made only a minimal effort to control her children until the store manager received a complaint from a customer, and told her that she needed to control her children. Anita was offended by the store manager's request, and left the store without buying anything, repeating, "They are just children having fun." Instead of Anita warning her children or leaving them at home with a sitter, she showed no regard to the store rules, the customers, or the safety of her children.

Many times, parents ignore and make excuses for their child's outbursts. Parents put up with bad behaviors too often. A child should always be reprimanded when they try to hit back at their parent, talk back or disrespectfully yell at them, or disregard their parental instruction. The parent may give you that look and say, "Oh they are just being cute, or they are just children." Or they may say to you, "You must not have any children." Regardless, if another individual has children or not, the cosigning of bad behavior should not be tolerated by a parent or a childcare provider. As a parent, by tolerating or ignoring this negative behavior, you are giving a "free pass" to your children that will make them believe that you accept and approve their poor social skills. This could cause long-term damage even if children are acting out negative behavior at an early age. As parents, we must not cosign our children's bad behavior.

"Protect yourself, your family, your investments, and guard all your interests."
Dr. Kim Logan-Nowlin

Chapter 6

What Does it Profit A Man to Gain Then Lose?

Gambling: To play games of chance for money. To stake or risk money or anything of value on the outcome of something involving chance.

Gambling is one of the strongest addictions. Ultimately, it is the loss of control that defines addictive behavior regardless of the substance or activity involved. According to an article by Karen Frazier on the *Love to Know* website, the National Council on Problem Gambling reports that approximately six million people ages 18 and older, and about a half a million teenagers are involved in some form of gambling. The reports show that youth are developing gambling addictions at a much higher rate than adults. Gambling is a problem for young adults, as well, with approximately six percent of college students in the US admitting they struggle with gambling issues.

Many homes and relationships are impacted, and even destroyed, by the addiction of gambling. Often gambling addicts have cross addictions that go together with gambling, such as smoking, drug use, and alcohol consumption. A gambling problem is analogous to cosigning bad behavior, because the gambling addict is determined to have "one more win" even though he knows that the odds are against him. The "I almost won" attitude is what keeps a gambler addicted to gambling and coming back for more. It will make the gambler empty his bank account, sell or pawn his valuables, and even risk losing his employment, just to play one more game.

Gambling addicts enable other gamblers. They meet, connect with strangers who are usually gamblers and supporters of the behavior, and become friends which helps justify their own negative actions. Here are some steps to assist in preventing the establishment of a gambling addiction:

1. Recognize and admit that you have an addiction.
2. Make a bold step and sign yourself out or take yourself out of a gambling establishment.
3. Stay away from any and all gambling houses, parties, and associations.
4. Seek professional counseling to address the gambling problem.

5. Do not participate in any games of chance—even lottery and raffle tickets or gambling games at amusement parks.
6. Do not participate in any event or activity that you must pay to play to win.

Gambling is considered a form of entertainment and not taken seriously. Because it doesn't cause physical harm, it is often looked at lightly or even ignored. Do not lend money to a gambler or even ask them to play or bet a few dollars for your own gain, because this is cosigning the bad behavior and your actions will be feeding the gambler's addiction.

"If you ignore bad behavior, you've endorsed it."
Dr. Kim Logan-Nowlin

Case Study: "No Looking Back"

Harold was a divorced, hardworking man, and employed with one of the major automotive manufacturing companies. He made a good living and had established a comfortable lifestyle. Harold was well respected and liked by his family and co-workers. However, there was one blemish on his seemingly normal lifestyle image. Harold was a habitual gambler. He often won big payouts, which contributed to him never realizing that he had a gambling problem and could not stop. His gambling addiction was masked by his winnings.

One day things changed for Harold, it was a day he never expected to come and one that he had not experienced as a gambler. He could not win for losing. No matter what game he played, no matter how little or how much he gambled, he could not win. Harold usually budgeted to only gamble $1,000 or less, which he would always bring with him. On that disappointing day, Harold lost it all and quickly. Even in those moments of loss, Harold believed that his winning streak was just one more card and one more dice throw away. Out of desperation, Harold did the unthinkable. He used all of his credit cards to get more money to gamble and withdrew $5,000 from his bank account with his debit card.

In three minutes, it was all gone. He returned to the ATM and withdrew more money from his checking account and lost that also. It wasn't until he had gambled $23,000 that Harold looked at his current reality, and said to himself, "This is not good. I need to get out of here and get some help." On his way out of the casino, Harold saw a sign posted that said, "If you need help with your gambling addiction, come see me." Harold went to the desk and asked the clerk for information about the gambling addiction sign. When it was explained to him, he asked to see a form that would prohibit a person from entering the casino due to gambling addiction problems. Without hesitation, Harold filled out the form, read it, signed it, and received a copy of it, and left the casino, never to return. Later the next day he called a counselor for help and enrolled in a gambling addiction class. Harold never gambled again, and he stopped cosigning his own bad behavior by making excuses.

"When one stands back and observes bad behavior and does nothing, he in turn is cosigning that act."
Dr. Kim Logan-Nowlin

Chapter 7

Inner Peace is Priceless

Peace of mind: A state of mental and emotional calmness with no worries or fear or stress.

How much is your peace of mind worth? The world is full of people who lack peace of mind, such as alcoholics, addicts, those who are incarcerated, homeless individuals, people who worry where their next meal is coming from, a parent laid off from their job, a person with a terminal illness, insomniacs, a spouse feeling guilty about their infidelity, an abused person, people who are fearful, and a person guilty of cosigning bad behavior. Without peace of mind it is difficult to remain focused in daily life, because a person's mind becomes overwhelmed when dealing with such difficult issues.

In some cases, there are good people who, for just one moment, made a poor decision to cosign a bad act or immoral behavior, and the weight of their guilt and shame has stolen their peace of mind. Others just simply enjoy wrong-doing. Fortunately, there are many people who do have a good conscience. Individuals with a good conscience and positive upbringing have a much greater sensitivity to the consequences associated with doing wrong or violating their morals and beliefs. It is not easy for a person with a good conscience to forgive themselves for a wrong act that he or she commits, because the guilt and the shame steals their peace of mind.

Some of the symptoms a guilty person experiences include insomnia, lack of appetite, inability to focus or do their job responsibilities, or lack of focus on their own needs or those of their family members. Guilt robs a person of their peace of mind, which happens to many people who cosign bad behavior. In spite of the fact that they thought the situation would be beneficial for them, the weight of the guilt of cosigning that bad behavior can become too overwhelming. Peace of mind is often lost and overtaken by guilt, and some have contemplated or even committed suicide.

Are you in the habit of denying yourself the peace your life is entitled to? What price can you put on your peace of mind if paralyzing feelings of guilt are a problem-area in your life? It is important for you to release the fear of peace. Does your peace depend on how your feelings are perceived by others? You deserve to be at peace in your relationships! It is time for you to realize the RACE Syndrome, and what guilt is doing to your personal peace.

The RACE Syndrome was developed by Arthur E. Nowlin, LMSW, to assist individuals and lead them to focus on positive decision-making. Identifying the RACE Syndrome also aims to confront and eliminate personal fears a person may experience in their life.

1. Rejection
2. Alienation
3. Complications
4. Experimentation

The RACE Syndrome defines the personal fear and anxiety that is hindering positive growth in the attitudes of men and women. Each letter stands for the following:

Rejection relates to fear and how it manifests itself in our relationships. Fear of rejection implies a person is not at peace in their relationships with others. True feelings cannot be shown when a person is filled with fear.

Alienation relates to a lack of trust. We develop a false sense of security in our personal domains, and as a result we do not want to let others get close to us.

Complications begin to move in on every aspect of our lives, because we have lost focus due to low self-esteem and the feelings of shame and guilt.

Experimentation is the area of major concern, because it leads a person to accept compromise and cosign negative behavior.

The RACE Syndrome prevents socialization skills from achieving their full potential and stagnates the opportunities for a person to become a positive influence on others. It brings awareness and support to people in their decision-making process. We do not have to fall prey or become a victim to negative behavior or people. The RACE Syndrome offers insight into mental health well-being and provides clarity for those who are looking for answers. It points to resolutions that can help a person move away from destructive behaviors in order to move forward with productive outcomes.

Each aspect of the RACE Syndrome helps an individual to admit, face, and overcome, fears in his or her life, so that it is possible to address the barriers and find relief and peace of mind. If trust has been violated, how can a person take the risk of restoration or find complete peace and trust within? This is a difficult process to go through, yet it is not impossible to receive total peace of mind. We must not cosign bad behavior through avoidance and silence and turn away from helping others and ourselves. We should follow the wise words in the Bible, which says, "Let us run with endurance the race God has set before us" Hebrews 12:1.

"Bad behavior can be given life and longevity if you cosign it."
Dr. Kim Logan-Nowlin

Case Study: "Peace Through a Storm"

Sometime ago my late husband, Arthur, and I had the pleasure of visiting an elderly man by the name of Mr. Paul Anthony. Mr. Anthony had been retired from his job for five years and lived on a fixed income. All his life he had cared for his family, and sadly, six months prior to our visit, his wife had passed away. He was a faithful man and strong in his convictions to the Lord. He always had a smile on his face, and had something good to say about everyone he met.

Mr. Anthony told us that one sunny afternoon there was a knock on the door. The visitor introduced himself as a representative from the Internal Revenue Service (IRS), and then he indicated that the house would be sold in 90 days to cover the payments for back taxes he owed. Knowing he had always paid his bills and taxes on time, Mr. Anthony became confused when the IRS representative asked for his past receipts. He did not know where the receipts were and was unable to find them. With that, he was given 90 days to pay or he would be forced to vacate the property.

After the man left, Mr. Anthony began to pray, He opened his line of communication to God and had faith. He knew without a doubt that he had paid the taxes. Almost three months went by, and, with only two days left, his neighbors grew concerned. Yet, in the face of the seriousness of the situation, Mr. Anthony kept his faith and cheerful countenance.

With only one day left, the IRS representative returned. Mr. Anthony stated, "I have one more day." The representative stated, "I know. I just came by to post a 'For Sale' sign on your lawn."

"Well then," was Mr. Anthony's response, "would you like to come in and have some tea?" Graciously, the man accepted. Mr. Anthony engaged in pleasant conversation, "Before my wife passed, she would make a very special herbal tea for me. I will make us some."

As he began to prepare the tea, he noticed old tea boxes on the shelf, and remembered his wife had kept important papers there. He began searching through the boxes and found the tax papers and receipts his wife had safely put away. Calmly, he went back to his guest, offered the tea and said, "I feel that you would find this to be interesting reading material, stamped with 'Taxes paid in full'."

The faith of Mr. Anthony was enough to keep him encouraged through a difficult time. He remained kind and polite in the midst of his storm, which allowed him to find the proof of payment that he had been seeking. We all have trials and tribulations throughout our lives. But what becomes important during these experiences is how strong our relationship with God is and not allowing anyone or anything to alter our inner peace.

"And let us not be weary in well-doing;
for in due season we shall reap, if we faint not."
Galatians 6:9

Chapter 8

Committed To Integrity

What do you do when you refuse to cosign negative behavior, but your efforts to discourage bad behavior seem to be in vain?

Integrity: The quality of being honest with yourself and others, and living a life that is aligned with your moral principles.

Developing personal integrity requires examining your beliefs, your value system, and taking conscious steps to behave in ways that are consistent with your personal moral code. The benefits of having a high level of integrity can be a tremendous advantage in the business world when you are applying for a job or seeking a promotion. Integrity can be a plus when you need the doors of opportunity opened or your voice to be heard. It can also be helpful in developing personal relationships. Even still, there are people with integrity who cosign bad behavior. Usually they compromise their integrity, morals, and belief system because they fear that they will lose an important relationship or position. Then there are others who are afraid to make things right after doing something wrong, because they fear that their integrity would be questioned in a negative light, so they choose to remain silent. There are still others who will take a risk and speak out in support of what is right and fair, because they believe that the cause and benefits are worth it.

The value of integrity is a very important characteristic to consider before cosigning any negative action. It is important to address our belief system regarding how we perceive integrity. But, what becomes difficult is implementing the behavior change that will improve how we evaluate ourselves and placing a priority on the value of integrity within our character development. In the process of understanding the mechanism we develop, it is most helpful if we become open to doing a personal inventory about who we are and how we cope with problems or negative experiences.

In many situations, we cope by avoidance, isolation, depression, and aggression. These methods for coping often create barriers in the way we interact with each other and prevent possible progress. We must be aware of the smallest detail regarding who we are as individuals, and how we present ourselves to others. Our attitude should reflect integrity, compassion, love, and not compromise honesty.

Here are ten principals of integrity that I have used personally, to help guide me to become a better person and one of high integrity.

1. Don't blame others for your mistakes.
2. Don't allow yourself to be involved in dishonest activities.
3. Hold yourself accountable.
4. Have all the facts before you make a decision.
5. Give 100% effort in everything you do and don't quit.
6. Truth is truth and it cannot be compromised.
7. Improve your self-awareness.
8. Write down your personal agreement and stick to it.
9. Surround yourself with people who share your same value system.
10. Learn to become comfortable with saying "No".

These principles can help to align yourself to improve on your decision-making approach and process. Integrity is the branch that connects a person's reputation to honesty and respect. When a person becomes disconnected from a positive value system and good standards of living, they tend to become involved in illegal activities that will have negative outcomes for their lives.

"Better is the poor that walketh in his integrity, than he that is perverse in his lips and is a fool."
Proverbs 19:1

Case Study: "Integrity Does Matter"

Carla was an employee of a major manufacturing company. Through hard work, determination, and commitment she earned her way up the corporate ladder to become the vice president of sales. Carla conducted all the important meetings of the North American Sales Divisions. During an audit of the computer purchases, Carla realized that one vendor had provided more computers than what was originally ordered. She reported this to the supervisor of the department.

Weeks later, Carla noticed once again that the companies were being undercharged for the equipment that her company had ordered. Carla again, mentioned it to the supervisors, but no action was taken. She reported it to the president of the company, and he told her just to ignore the discrepancy. Carla stated she could not, and had to report it to the company and the necessary authorities.

Carla was fired from her position for insubordination, maintaining her honesty, and demonstrating her commitment to stand for what is right. Carla was not going to jeopardize her livelihood or her reputation for money. She later filed a lawsuit against the company for wrongful discharge. The company board of directors terminated the president and the supervisor. Carla was reinstated as vice president of operations with an increase in her salary and with full benefits. Carla never wavered from her convictions and moral beliefs, and she continued to be honest, truthful, and fair.

"Thou shalt not steal."
Exodus 20:15

Chapter 9

Standing On Honesty

Honesty: Uprightness of character or actions.

Honesty implies a refusal to lie, steal, or deceive in any way. Honor suggests an active or anxious regard for the standards of one's profession, calling, or position. Integrity implies trustworthiness and incorruptibility to a degree that one is incapable of being false to a trust, responsibility, or pledge.

It is important to be honest with yourself, so that you can require that characteristic of others, too. Honesty creates an atmosphere of love, trustworthiness, and it attracts honesty and prevents you from cosigning bad behavior. Honesty allows you to take responsibility for acts of omission, mistakes, and shortcomings.

Imagine being terminated over two payroll violations. In the beginning or the end of a shift, a few minutes may not appear to be a major issue or concern at the time, until it is brought to the attention of your leader. What seems like nothing, becomes a concern when the supervisor recognizes on multiple occasions that an employee's time was not accurately recorded. Falsifying time, even if it is a couple of minutes, is the same as telling a lie. It is dangerous to have the mindset that it is only a little lie, no big deal, and no one will know it is missing. The bottom line is that it is dishonesty and cheating. When multiplied, over a period of time, those couple of minutes of time can add up to hundreds and thousands of dollars.

A "little" lie can later turn into a couple standing in divorce court, or someone facing incarceration. Dishonesty and cheating are bad behaviors that can have long-term effects, damage reputations, and, in the work place, can lead to disciplinary actions even up to discharge. Is ten minutes of time or that lie worth it? When your means of support, family, health, or employment can be affected, you may want to ask yourself to look at the big picture of the consequences. "Is this really worth it?" Ask yourself first, "What is the worst possible outcome that could take place by the decision that I am about to make? Do I really want to cosign this?

"A lie cannot be measured by size or appearance but only by truth."
Dr. Kim Logan-Nowlin

Case Study: "Missing the Bigger Picture"

Sally and Joe worked together in a clothing store. Customer traffic was usually very slow during the last half hour of the day. One person could operate the store at that time, if necessary. Sally wanted to avoid rush-hour traffic, so she asked Joe if he would mind if she left 30 minutes early. Joe agreed, because he knew he could handle the very few customers who came in right before the store closed each day. Sally began to leave early frequently, and Joe continued to cover for her.

One day the boss called the store to speak to Sally, but she had already left the store. The boss asked why he was not notified that Sally needed to leave early that day, and he was concerned that maybe she had a family emergency. When the manager checked his time reports at the end of the week, he noticed that there were no adjustments on her timesheet showing the times she had left early during the week.

With Joe being the team leader, he was questioned by the manager as to why he was not reporting this to him? When Sally was questioned about leaving early, she stated, "Joe always allows me to leave early to avoid the rush hour traffic, and he never said it was a problem as long as business was slow." The problem was that her absence from work was not reflected on her payroll sheet. Sally was terminated for falsifying time sheets, and Joe was terminated for cosigning and approving it.

*"Extortion turns a wise person into a fool,
and a bribe corrupts the heart."*
Ecclesiastes 7:7

Chapter 10

Blackmailed To Cosign

What do you do when you are pressured or coerced to cosign?

Coerced: To persuade an unwilling person to do something by using force or threats.

In the political arena, there are questionable politicians who use their authority, position, power, threats, and name recognition to influence or obtain certain favors or support. Politicians may promise to lobby, award contracts, and promote and legislate bills to be signed and passed. Greed and self-interest are primary reasons for corruption within the political arena.

Negative perception continues to be associated with politics, because the actions of corrupt politicians create fear and intimidation within our communities. However, there are politicians who will not cosign negative behavior or compromise their morals or belief system. These individuals promote justice, integrity, and fairness through their political position. They utilize their opportunities to speak up for what is right and strive to uphold laws and policies which will be beneficial for their constituents. They discredit any cosigners of negative behavior. If and when we choose to remain silent about things that are wrong, we are like the corrupt politicians—guilty by omission.

Money and power are the life blood of corruption in the political arena. Political corruption is the use of power by government officials or their network contacts for illegitimate, private gain. Forms of corruption vary, but include: embezzlement, influence peddling, nepotism, extortion, bribery, cronyism, graft, fraud, parochialism, and patronage. Consequences of political corruption can have major, expensive, and long-term negative effects on people. The bad behavior undermines political efficacy, distorts representation in policy making, questions the legitimacy of government, and falsifies the democratic values of trust and tolerance. The effects are far reaching, even causing increases in cost of goods and services and the government provisions of those services. Political corruption is a major contributor to citizens losing faith and confidence in government officials. Some of the political figures, who were voted into office based on their promises to bring about change, improvement, prosperity, and better living conditions, are the very ones who are greedy and steal the funds allocated to improve conditions in their areas of influence.

Corrupt behaviors often cause citizens to avoid becoming involved in civic affairs, lose faith in the voting system, and therefore, open the door for even more corrupt minded people to enter government. The lack of faith in the system and the stealing of tax money can have a tremendous negative effect on small businesses and the welfare of the entire city. Funding for health projects, safety, road repair, school assistance is greatly impacted by political corruption. Many tax dollars and financial contributions are lining the pockets of the corrupt and greedy politicians. Sadly, many others know about it but believe that in order to maintain their position and remain in the influential, powerful political inner circles, some chose to stay silent, making them guilty by omission. The consequences of dishonesty and betrayal of trust hurts everyone. Reputations get damaged and faith in the system is destroyed as the people suffer. We must take a position of honesty and integrity in order to represent all people in truth, honesty, and justice. The right to vote for our elected officials is one of the greatest privileges that we have in the US. The benefits of being elected to represent a group of people should never be abused.

"Just because you are not exposed or found guilty, does not make you innocent."
Dr. Kim Logan-Nowlin

Case Study: "Paid in Full"

A political figure entered a popular five-star restaurant with several members of his entourage. They sat down to dine, ordered a wonderful meal, and received outstanding service. When they finished eating their meal, they preceded to just walk out of the restaurant without paying their bill. As the political figure passed the stunned waiter, he said, "The bill is all covered and don't worry about it." The waiter felt uncomfortable with the response from the politician because of the large charge on the bill.

Before the party could exit out of the door, the waiter notified the owner who was in his office. The owner hurried out and said to the party, "I don't understand why you are leaving. Was there a problem with the food or service?" The politician turned and whispered to the owner, "Listen, unless you want your city license revoked you better learn how to play the game and take care of this bill." The owner, feeling intimidated and threatened, contacted his attorney and the television media to share his story.

When the story became headline news soon after, a check was delivered for the full amount, including a generous tip with an apology, claiming that it was all a misunderstanding. Unfortunately, this was a common practice of this unscrupulous political figure, but this restaurant owner refused to cosign his bad behavior even in the face of fear and intimidation.

"To whom much is given much is required."
Luke 12:48

Chapter 11

No More Secrets

Secrets: Thoughts or experiences not known, seen, or not meant to be known by others.

People keep secrets because they want information to remain private, to prevent shame or embarrassment, or because they may feel that the situation is not a concern of anyone else. From a positive perspective, secrets create an element of surprise like when a birthday party or marriage proposal is planned. Unfortunately, other types of secrets are often harmful, embarrassing, and, when discovered in an intimate relationship, can contribute to verbal and physical abuse.

The effort required to maintain a secret can be emotionally stressful and draining. It causes a person to feel ingenuine and like a pretender to those who they are keeping the secret from for fear that it may be disclosed. Some people in relationships keep secrets from others and even from close family members.

Another reason secret-keeping is harmful is due to the risk of losing someone who is important or valuable in a person's life as a result of the betrayal of trust, broken commitment, or unkept vow. If a secret gets out before the right time, or if it is never intended to be known, it can create tremendous hardship. Some secrets, when discovered, can be very difficult to accept and recover from.

Emotional or mental abuse can be just as damaging as physical abuse. Nonverbal communication can send signals to the abused individual that threatens them and forces them to not say or do something. The person who is the abuser wants to maintain control over the victim silently in order to maintain the appearance of innocence and to avoid shame and guilt.

In domestic violence, gaslighting is a common form of psychological manipulation. It is used to control another individual's thought process. According to *Psychology Today* contributor and professor, Preston Ni, "Gaslighting is a form of persistent manipulation and brainwashing that causes the victim to doubt her or himself, and ultimately lose her or his own sense of perception, identity, and self-worth. The term is derived from the 1944 film *Gaslight,* in which a husband tries to convince his wife that she's insane by causing her to question herself and her reality".

Gaslighting is an extremely effective form of emotional abuse that causes a victim to question their own feelings, instincts, and sanity, which gives the abusive partner a lot of power (and we know that abuse is about power and control). Once an abusive partner has broken down the victim's ability to trust their own perceptions, the victim is more likely to stay in the abusive relationship. When someone has knowledge of an abusive situation, and they ignore the bad behavior because there is some form of personal gain or benefit for themselves, then they are choosing to support the abuser and they are cosigning the bad behavior.

In an article on the *Psychology Today* website entitled "7 Stages of Gaslighting in a Relationship" Ni describes gaslighting in the following seven categories:

1. Lie and Exaggerate. The person who is gaslighting makes up generalized false narratives and accusations about the gaslightee, putting them on the defensive. They may say something like, "You don't know what you are doing, that is why your idea didn't work."

2. Repetition. Saying the same negative statements constantly is a type of psychological warfare that keeps the lies alive and is a method the gaslighter uses to try to maintain control of the relationship and feel dominant over the gaslightee.

3. Escalate When Challenged. If the gaslighter is told they are lying, they spread twice or three times as many falsehoods, emphasize blame on the gaslightee even more than they had previously done, and use emphatic denial to create doubt and confusion in the situation.

4. Wear Out the Victim. Through the persistent attacks, the gaslighter slowly wears down the victim, to the point when the gaslightee actually questions their own perspective and identity. The victim "becomes discouraged, resigned, pessimistic, fearful, debilitated, and self-doubting," says Ni.

5. Form Codependent Relationships. When we discuss codependency, we are referring to the experience a person has when they rely excessively on another person for their emotional or psychological well-being. A gaslighter will use codependency to turn the gaslightee into a type of puppet. They will place themselves in the position of "power to grant acceptance, approval, respect, safety, and security" says Ni. "A codependent relationship is formed based on fear, vulnerability, and marginalization."

6. Give False Hope. While manipulating the victim, a gaslighter will give the victim little reasons to hope or feel safe by showing them temporary kindness or even voicing regret for how they have behaved. These momentary displays of moderation make the victim think, "This isn't so bad, or things are getting better."

7. Dominate and Control. Professor Ni says, "At its extreme, the ultimate objective of a pathological gaslighter is to control, dominate, and take advantage of another individual, or a group, or even an entire society." The gaslighter uses continuous lies and coercion to place their victim in a state of fear and confusion, with the ultimate goal—subordination.

I do have the power to say, "No more!"
Dr. Kim Logan-Nowlin

DOMESTIC VIOLENCE STATISTICS

According to the National Coalition Against Domestic Violence website, every year, more than 10 million men and women in the U.S. are victims of domestic violence. Its impact can be felt far and wide. The following statistics were reported on the Social Solutions Blog in 2018.

—About 36% of women and about 29% of men in the U.S. report having experienced rape, physical violence, and/or stalking by an intimate partner in their lifetime.

—Each minute, about 20 individuals in the U.S. are being abused by an intimate partner every year, which adds up to more than 10 million women and men.

—Nearly 1 in 4 women and 1 in 7 men were reported as victims of severe physical violence by an intimate partner during their lifetime.

—Out of all the types of violent crimes, intimate partner violence accounts for 15% overall.

—Intimate partner violence was a factor in 40% of female homicides in 15 states.

—Out of all cases where domestic violence takes place, 85% are against females, and 15% are against males.

—There is a 40% higher risk for intimate partner violence among women who have a disability.

—Domestic violence cases were reported by 63% of all homeless women.

—Domestic violence is reported as a cause of homelessness among 28% of destitute families.

—About 50% of all adults in the U.S. are likely to be victim to an intimate partner's psychological aggression at some point in their life.

—Children are being exposed to domestic violence at a rate of about 5 million per year.

—These children are more likely to become suicidal, get addicted to drugs or alcohol, become a teenage prostitute, or commit rape.

—According to a report from The Center for Violence-Free Relationships, 40% of all domestic violence cases involve families with children under the age of 18.

—Reports show that 50% of individuals who are battering a spouse or significant other are also abusing their children.

—Men, in all parts of the world, who experienced domestic abuse as children are 3-4 times more likely to commit violence against an intimate partner in their adulthood.

—Studies show that 81% of women and 35% of men who experienced intimate partner rape, stalking, or physical violence were impacted by short-term and long-term post-traumatic stress disorder and injuries.

—During the course of a year, 4% of high school students reported being intentionally hit, forcefully pushed, or physically hurt by their boyfriend or girlfriend.

—About 1 in 3 people who are domestic violence victims receive medical treatment for their injuries.

—The majority of domestic violence cases are not officially documented, and men are less likely than women to report their situation to the police.

The problem with domestic violence needs to be addressed. Until the numbers are at zero percent, it will always be too many. Not one individual deserves to be physically, emotionally, and verbally abused. There is a better way to live, and it should involve removing themselves from a negative situation until the problem is addressed and resolved through professional counseling. If safety is a risk factor, the victim must leave the dangerous environment. Creating some space is the best way to avoid feeding into the negative situation, and, most importantly, the victim must protect themself.

"Abuse is a characteristic of hate and control.
Love has no part in it."
Dr. Kim Logan-Nowlin

Case Study: "No More Fear"

Seventeen-year-old Elizabeth traveled to California for her summer break to visit with her cousin Ashley who was also seventeen years of age. They both were so excited about their summer vacation plans and seeing one another. Upon her arrival, Elizabeth was greeted at the airport by Ashley and her family, and they were all so happy to see her. After getting settled into their home, she and Ashley went out to see a movie with some of her friends.

Ashley's boyfriend Charles was nineteen years of age and a college student. He invited his friend Tony to come along to meet Elizabeth. During the movie, Elizabeth overheard, Charles and Ashley arguing, and saw Charles grab Ashley by the arm, leaving a bruise on her. Ashley tried to play it off as though it was no big deal. Later during the evening, Charles again grabbed her but this time he also punched her in the stomach, thinking that no one had seen him do it. Ashley got up to go to the restroom, but Charles told her to sit down. Elizabeth noticed that Charles had a great amount of control over Ashley. Tony had not seen any of the negative behaviors committed, because he was so engrossed in the movie.

After the movie was over, Elizabeth tried to talk to Ashley, but Charles would not let Ashley near her. He whispered something into her ear, and she wiped away a tear and walked to the car. After the date, Charles and Tony took the girls back home. Charles gave Ashley a goodbye kiss as if nothing unusual had happened. During the night, Ashley was very quiet, but Elizabeth could hear her crying. Charles was calling her on her cellphone all night. Elizabeth could hear him screaming and telling her not to say anything about the bruise or how he had punched her.

In one of Elizabeth's classes at school, she had been studying about sexual abuse and domestic violence. Now, and up close, she was seeing and experiencing the fact that her cousin Ashley was a victim of domestic violence. During the earlier hours of the morning, Ashley finally told Elizabeth what had been happening for the past two years, and disclosed the abuse that she had suffered from Charles. She told Elizabeth, "He is not a bad person when he is not angry. He is a wonderful guy." Ashley's parents had no idea that their daughter was being abused. Ashley knew that her parents would make her stop seeing him and would possibly press charges. Ashley was so in love with Charles, that she always made excuses for his abusive ways, and, by doing so, she cosigned his bad behavior and violent acts.

Ashley also told Elizabeth that Charles had gotten her pregnant twice, and each time he had insisted that she have an abortion. Charles was so controlling of Ashley that he would not let her join the band or the cheer team at school. She had hidden the truth by telling her parents that she had lost interest in the school activities. Charles often followed her home from school, and told her that when she turned eighteen, she was going to move out of her parent's home and would be moving into his apartment.

Elizabeth knew she had to do something, because she realized that Ashley was no longer making decisions for herself and her own happiness. By remaining silent, Ashley was giving more power to Charles, and it could endanger her life. Elizabeth broke her silence and told her aunt and uncle what had been going on for the past two years. They filed a protective order against Charles and banned Ashley from seeing him. Ashley was so angry at Elizabeth, but she later realized that it was in her best interest, because she did not have the courage to stand up to Charles. From that day forward, she no longer cosigned the negative behaviors of Charles.

In many cases of sexual abuse or domestic violence, the victim will take responsibility for the actual abuse they are experiencing from the perpetrator. According to Justin Leader, vice president of business development with Benefit Design Specialists, Inc., the Stockholm Syndrome, or capture-bonding, is a psychological phenomenon described in 1973. It is described as the experience a hostage has when they begin to express empathy and sympathy towards their captor. They start to have positive feelings for their captors and even defend them and sympathize with them. Types of victims who are usually experiencing the Stockholm Syndrome are the following:

- Abused children
- Battered/Abused women
- Prisoners of war
- Cult members
- Incest victims
- Criminal hostage captives
- Concentration camp prisoners
- Individuals in controlling/intimidating relationships

In the final analysis, emotionally bonding with an abuser is actually a strategy for survival for victims of abuse and intimidation. The Stockholm Syndrome can also be found in family, romantic, and interpersonal relationships. The abuser may be a spouse, boyfriend or girlfriend, parent, or major role where the abuser is in a position of control or authority.

To understand the components of Stockholm Syndrome as it relates to abusive and controlling relationships is very critical. Once the syndrome is understood, it's easy to understand why victims support, love, and even defend their abusers and controllers. In order for a person to change, they first must recognize that they need to change. Then they begin to develop a desire to change. That desire brings about a renewing of their thought processes, and a desire to associate with like-minded people who dislike wrongdoing. It is a good idea to seek creditable counseling, find mentors, spend an increasing amount of time in prayer, which will result in greater faith in God. Claim the promise in Proverbs 3:5-7, "Trust in the Lord with all thine heart and lean not unto thine own understanding. In all thy ways acknowledge Him, and He shall direct thy paths. Be not wise in thine own eyes; fear the Lord and depart from evil."

"My people are destroyed for a lack of knowledge."
Hosea 4:6

Chapter 12

"... Even In The Church!"

Surprisingly, one of the most common places where cosigning bad behavior exists is in the church. Bad behavior and sinful living are closely related. Negative lifestyles in the church are constantly practiced, while the vision of the pastor is often ignored. Sadly, fornication, adulterous relationships, sexual abuse, and theft of money are bad behaviors that often take place at a high level. These acts should be reported to the church leadership in order to prevent further discourse among the membership.

Some churches seem to operate like a weekend social club gathering, rather than maintaining the reverence and order of a house of worship, therefore many of these sinful acts are not taken seriously. These things are sometimes kept in-house among the members. These types of situations, are examples of how church members and ministry leaders witness and cosign bad behavior.

Frequently, the noted behaviors did not start yesterday. However, there are ministry leaders, that have continued to ignore the red flags of sin and inappropriate, bad behavior. For example, imagine you are a single woman sitting in church and you receive a text message from a married man sitting on another pew; or the deacon takes $20 out of the offering plate; or a woman intentionally wears a tight short skirt with a low-cut v-neck blouse trying to entice the pastor and other men in the church; or inappropriate hugging and kissing takes place under the guise of a "holy kiss" expressing Christian love.

Let the record show that this is not indicative of all churches. Sin exists everywhere and mainly resides in the hearts of people. The church house is not exempt from sin, sinners, or bad behavior. How do we recognize and address these issues that plague the church? There are passages in the Bible that speak about the cosigning of bad behavior by church leaders. One situation in the Old Testament is subtitled, "The Lord's Case Against Israel". Hosea 4:6 states, "My people perish because of the lack of knowledge." God blamed the sinful-living lifestyles that existed in Israel on the priests, because they did not tell the people about God's Word and the error of their ways. The priest's refusal to acknowledge the revelation of God, caused God to punish the people and the land. The plants, the birds, and the fish were dying off. The people practiced sexual immorality and worshipped idols. They were cursing, lying, killing, stealing from one another, and having loose sex. Because the priests were also sinning, even the prophets started to sin like them. The consequence of their refusal to acknowledge God and His Word was that their lust and desires would never be satisfied.

Many of the people were constantly in a drunken stupor, and they were worshipping and talking to wooden idols. The priests were cosigning bad behavior, and God punished them. They were enjoying and benefiting from the pleasures of sinful living. When the priest complained about the sins of the people, God said (paraphrase), "Don't point your finger at someone else and try to pass the blame, I blame you! I refuse to recognize you as my priest."

This same type of behavior is happening in today's society. People are practicing and cosigning bad behavior. People are ignoring and refusing morality, wisdom, and good counseling because of their strong desire and lust for personal pleasure, fame, fortune, and power. They cosign these behaviors, because, many times, they want the same thing and get caught up in the moment and the pleasure. True Christians hate sin, but some continue to cosign or ignore sinful lifestyles and bad behavior in the church. Ask yourself, as you sit in service watching, as well as praying, "Am I cosigning any bad behavior in my church?" God loves everyone, and Jesus surrendered His life on the cross so that all may be saved. God's intention is for us not to stand in judgment of others, but to show love and help those in need. However, we cannot cosign bad behavior within the church.

*"But if you warn righteous people not to sin
and they listen to you and do not sin,
they will live, and you will have saved yourself, too."*
Ezekiel 3:21 NLT

Case Study: "Driven to Change"

Mitchell Peterson was a van driver for the church. He had been a loyal driver for twelve years, picking up the seniors who did not have transportation. He took the van home on Saturday night so he could get up early the next morning to pick up the members on time. Each morning before service, he got in the church van, and drove to a nearby restaurant to have breakfast, and after service he would take the members home. After he completed his transportation services, he would go and visit his family and have Sunday dinner. Mitchell did not know that there were some church members who lived in his family's neighborhood and worked in the mall where he often shopped.

One day, one of the members saw him at church, and asked him to have a private conversation with him. The member told Mitchell that using the church van for private and personal business could cause liability issues for the church, and if an accident took place while he was using the van for personal errands, it would cost Mitchell his job. Mitchell was defensive at first, but, later that night while watching the news, he saw an accident involving a van and a car. He realized that, while using the church van for personal reasons was also causing undue wear and tear on the vehicle, an accident would be the worst thing that could happen.

Mitchell called the church member, apologized, and donated money to the transportation fund to cover any vehicle expenses he might have contributed to during those personal trips to town. He never used the van for personal use again. It was the member's decision to not cosign Mitchell's behavior by speaking out against his selfish and costly act.

"Listen to advice and accept correction."
Proverbs 19:20

Chapter 13

Vision Of Excellence

Final thoughts and personal reflections . . .

Throughout my life, I have experienced and have been guilty myself of exercising poor decision making and bad behavior from my childhood and into my adulthood. Experience can be the best teacher, especially if you do not consider the consequences. What is the worst outcome that can happen as a result of the decision that you are going to make? You need to ask yourself that question in most decision-making situations. Are you mentally, physically, or emotionally prepared and capable of handling the possible outcomes?

Refrain from wrong-doing, because every negative situation has a beginning. Your decision to participate in negative behavior through action or silence will give life to bad behavior. In many instances, individuals try to justify right over wrong. There are those who are looking for short cuts to success. Some want to take the law into their own hands and try to obtain power by any means. One of those means is cosigning bad behavior.

When you take a close look at our society, many people want happiness, success, and justice. However, the lack of patience and resources and a desire to be accepted causes people to follow and support individuals and their bad character. Their support is primarily assisted by cosigners of the bad behavior. Becoming a difference-maker and an example of good behavior, excellent moral principles, and honest integrity, can help to eliminate the corruption within someone's heart. You can be that light and example by standing up for what is right, not having any role in wrong behavior, and refusing to associate with anyone or any circumstance that could jeopardize your good name.

Reflecting back over my life as a Christian, wife, mother, therapist/counselor, professor, TV host, entrepreneur, and published author, it is vital for me to take, on a daily basis, a personal inventory regarding my decision-making processes and to not allow myself to cosign bad behavior. I pride myself in operating with honesty and integrity, putting that before financial gain, popularity, or power. I have seen many of my brilliant colleagues fall by the wayside, stripped of their credentials and professional licenses, because they were seeking that fast lane to success.

Mainly by omission, we support bad morals, behavior, and poor leadership throughout our political arena. We see the negative coercion of blackmail and intimidation, and we fall silently by the wayside and give a pass to continued corruption. These people are just as guilty as those who committed the act.

In our homes we allow our children to be disrespectful, live in our house while not contributing anything, and some parents eventually give their adult children a pass to take advantage of their hard work and effort. Some parents are also guilty, and must stop making excuses for their children, which is another example of cosigning bad behavior. Having inappropriate affairs, married or single, can cause destruction of relationships and trust. Even at times, one's life can be put in danger from having an inappropriate or emotional affair.

People need to be aware of the possible consequences or outcomes of their decisions, hesitate, and refuse to participate, contribute to, or remain silent about negative and bad behavior. There are many counseling tools that could help an individual address their concerns regarding cosigning bad behavior.

- Prayer
- Speak up and speak out
- Notify authorities
- Refuse to compromise
- Offer positive advice
- Suggest psychological counseling
- Separate from the perpetrator
- Have courage to address and expose the negative behavior

- Set realistic boundaries
- Surround yourself with healthy and positive people

We all have the right to make choices about what we believe or what we become a part of. It is foolish to be a part of something that you do not believe in. My advice to you, as a professional licensed therapist/counselor, is to first think thoroughly before you act. Don't become involved or lend a hand in negative, bad behavior. Don't cosign or give the impression of approval, and, definitely, do not remain silent. When a situation arises and you can cosign bad behavior, please—do not pick up the pen!

"Misery loves company.
It does not need your help, or permission,
and it certainly does not need your signature.
Don't pick up the pen."
Dr. Kim Logan-Nowlin

Case Study: "The Price Was NOT Right"

Robert and Melody Lacey were a happily married couple and the proud parents of one son, Robert Jr., an 18-year-old high school graduate. The Lacey's were highly educated and successful business owners. Both he and his wife graduated from a major university and came from prestigious families.

Mr. Lacey was concerned that his son would not qualify to attend his alma mater, and this troubled him for several months. One afternoon Mr. Lacey was having lunch with a business associate. The associate asked him what was troubling him. Mr. Lacey stated that his son was not accepted to the school of his choice, and it was very embarrassing to the family. The associate replied to him, "I have the answer to your problem. He stated that for a certain fee we can have your son admitted into the school of your choice, and we have all the necessary people in place to get it done." He also stated that for an additional cost they can guarantee that his son will be in the top ten percent of his class. Mr. Lacey agreed to the cost of $150,000 to secure his son's placement in the school and the guarantee that he will graduate with honors.

A few months later the process for his admittance was in motion. When Mrs. Lacey found out about this scheme, she was so upset about what her husband had done. She told her husband that she would not cosign on this behavior and that she could not believe he would stoop to this level of dishonesty. She also told her husband that she would not go to prison over this or involve her son. She said that this is not worth the damage that you will do to our reputation in the community. Mrs. Lacey warned her husband that if he did not stop these illegal actions, that she would contact the school authorities.

After much thought, Mr. Lacey realized that the actions he was considering doing were criminal and were not worth the risk and the possible consequences of such dishonesty and deceit. He cancelled the arrangement even losing his down payment. The Lacey's immediately enrolled Robert Jr. into a local community college. Mr. Lacey apologized and thanked his wife for helping him to keep a level head. He decided to accept his son where he was academically.

After the first year of school, Robert Jr. made the dean's list with a 4.0 GPA and with 16 credits. He majored in business to work with his father and carry on the family legacy. After two years in community college maintaining a 4.0 GPA, Robert applied to his father's alma mater and was accepted on his own merit and brought his father to tears. His father learned a valuable lesson and his wife's decision not to cosign criminal and dishonest behavior saved his family from shame and embarrassment. Robert Jr. completed his undergraduate degree and earned his MBA and now works with his parents in operating the family business.

*"He who passively accepts evil is as much involved in it
as he who helps to perpetrate it.
He who accepts evil without protesting against it
is really cooperating with it"*
Martin Luther King, Jr.

NOTE TO COSIGNER

"When you finish reading the contract below, my professional advice to you as it relates to cosigning bad behavior is . . . Don't pick up the pen, your signature is not wanted."

Dr. Kim Logan-Nowlin

Bad Behavior Contract

I, the undersigned, knowingly and willingly, support the following behaviors either by commission or omission:

- Inappropriate relationships
- Illegal activities
- Unhealthy lifestyles
- Dangerous and destructive habits
- Poor eating habits
- Unsafe & poor safety practices
- Lying
- Dishonesty/Cheating
- Bullying/Fighting/Road rage
- Greed

Sign_____

Cosigner_____

Questions to be considered if you are a cosigner of bad behavior:

Am I aware of bad behavior taking place in my life?
☐ Yes ☐ No
Am I aware of the consequences of the possible negative outcome of this behavior?
☐ Yes ☐ No
Is this behavior dishonest?
☐ Yes ☐ No
Do you enable other people to demonstrate bad behavior?
☐ Yes ☐ No
Do you ignore the bad behavior?
☐ Yes ☐ No
Are you aware why you choose to remain silent when you see bad behavior?
☐ Yes ☐ No
Do you practice bad behavior?
☐ Yes ☐ No

If you answered yes to any of these questions, then you are guilty of cosigning bad behavior by commission or omission and your name belongs on the contract that is on the previous page.

"Guilty by Omission."

*"When one stands back and observes the bad behavior
and does not do anything,
he in turn is cosigning that act.
When you see something and know better,
and choose not to do or say anything,
you have cosigned that act of bad behavior."*
Dr. Kim Logan-Nowlin

*"Cosigning is a way of supporting or ensuring against unexpected failure.
Be mindful of who and what you cosign."*
Dr. Kim Logan-Nowlin

Bibliography

"20 Alarming Domestic Violence Statistics for 2018." *Social Solutions Blog,* https://www.socialsolutions.com/blog/domestic-violence-statistics-2018.

DiClement, CC; Prochaska, JO. "In Search of How People Change: Applications to Addictive Behaviors." *The American Psychologist,* vol. 47, no. 9, September 1992, pp. 1102-14.

Frazier, Karen. "Gambling Addiction Statistics." *Love to Know,* https://addiction.lovetoknow.com/wiki/Gambling_Addiction_Statistics.

Jeirles, Summer. "Why do People Enable?" *American Counseling Association,* https://www.counseling.org/news/aca-blogs/aca-member-blogs/aca-member-blogs/2016/07/18/why-do-people-enable. July 18, 2016.

Kuhn, T.S. *The structure of scientific revolutions.* Chicago University. Chicago Press, 1962.

Leader, Justin. "Healthcare Stockholm Syndrome." Benefit Design Specialists, Inc. https://bdsadmin.com/about-us. April 26, 2016

Ni, Preston. "7 Stages of Gaslighting in a Relationship." *Psychology Today*, https://www.psychologytoday.com/intl/blog/communication-success/201704/7-stages-gaslighting-in-relationship. April 30, 2017.

Ni, Preston. "Gaslighting: How it Manipulates Relationships." *Psychology Today*, https://www.psychologytoday.com/us/blog/communication-success/201707/gaslighting-how-it-manipulates-relationships. July 9, 2017.

"Statistics" *National Coalition Against Domestic Violence,* https://ncadv.org/statistics.

Reader Reflections

Reader Reflections

Reader Reflections

Reader Reflections

"The measure of intelligence is the ability to change."
Albert Einstein

Author's Bio

DR. KIM LOGAN-NOWLIN

**Entrepreneur • Speaker • Author •
Clinical Psychotherapist/Counselor •
Executive Life Coach • TV Host**

Kim Logan-Nowlin, Ph.D., LPC, BCPC, ACAC, IAMFC, MFT, AAFLP or "Dr. Kim," as she is affectionately called by audiences, is a dynamic speaker who always leaves her audiences spellbound. Dr. Kim was recently named one of the top three marriage counselors in Detroit on September 13, 2018 by Three Best Rated Company. As President/ CEO of Kim Logan-Nowlin Communications, Inc. for over 38 years, she has trained and counseled people from all walks of life to be **inspired** and to recognize how your words can change your choices and your life. She holds a Bachelor of Science Degree in Special Education, Master of Arts Degree in Family and Guidance Counseling, and a Doctorate of Philosophy Degree in Oral and Interpersonal Communication and Clinical Family Counseling. Dr. Kim is certified in AIDS prevention, substance abuse therapy, and sex abuse counseling. She is also a certified sign language interpreter for the deaf.

 Dr. Kim has served as family life leader, praise and worship leader, minister of music, and stewardship leader of her local church, the City Temple Seventh-day Adventist Church, located in Detroit, Michigan. Dr. Kim enjoys working with the youth throughout the world and serving as a facilitator for the United Youth Congresses, youth federations, camp meetings, marriage retreats/conferences, schools, graduations, community-based organizations, churches, and many other roles. Dr. Kim is the founder and directress of God's Hands of Praise Gospel Sign Language Ministry established in 1994. She continues to minister with her choir to help bring joy to the hearing and the hearing challenged. Dr. Kim is known across the world for her drama presentations during her sermons, seminars, and workshops that help to bring insight and understanding to her audiences.

Author's Bio

Dr. Kim is a proud Alumni of Oakwood College (University) in Huntsville, Alabama, and Wayne State University in Detroit, Michigan. Dr. Logan-Nowlin also serves as the Oakwood University Detroit Chapter Membership Chair. Dr. Kim also serves as Professor of Speech Communication, Theater, and Sign Language for Wayne County Community College District.

As a national inspirational/motivational speaker, her oratory brings encouragement, direction, hope, and healing to thousands each year as she travels around the U.S. and abroad sharing words of inspiration for all ages. She is a gifted woman on a mission to help others discover their gifts. She has been granted hundreds of awards for her achievements and community service. Dr. Logan-Nowlin has conducted conferences, seminars, radio programs, television shows, and has been teaching the importance of living to be well for over 38 years. Dr. Kim is the host of Facebook Live events called "Live 2 Be Well" every Tuesday night at 9:15 p.m. and other social media outlets.

Along with her late husband and professional therapist, Arthur Nowlin, LMSW, CAADC, AAFLP, they have met and she continues to meet the needs of hurting individuals and families as Christian family therapists and counselors in their private practice in Detroit, Michigan. The Nowlin's served as co-directors of the family life department of the Lake Region Conference from 2007-2014. They also served as the co-hosts of *Making It Work* on 3ABN Dare to Dream Television Network. In the Fall of 2017, *Live to Be Well with Dr. Kim* aired on the same network. Dr. Kim joined a newly developed TV program in Detroit entitled "The Girls Group" in October 2018.

Dr. Kim and her late husband Arthur E. Nowlin, have authored six published books:

The Attitude Adjustment of the Christian Man and Woman

Refusing A Direct Order

Friends in the Bedroom, But Strangers in Church

Marriage: Living With the Unexplainable

Intensive Care: Can My Marriage Survive or Not?

Dr. Kim continues to speak nationally, author books, and be a contributing writer for *Message Magazine* ("The Drama Files" and "Bounce Back Relationship Articles"). Dr. Kim is the founder and director of the "Live 2 Be Well" organization which serves to help, develop, and inspire all people to have a balanced life with mind, body, and soul. Dr. Logan-Nowlin's motto is: "To inspire others to aspire to live to be well"

www.drkiminspires.com

KIM LOGAN-NOWLIN AUTHOR, SPEAKER, TRAINER

Other Featured Books

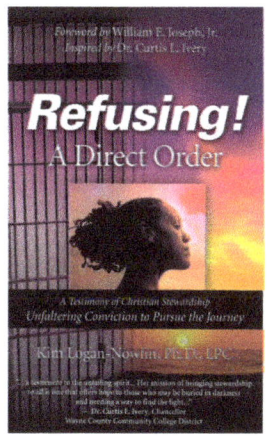

Refusing! A Direct Order
A Personal Testimony of Christian Stewardship:
Unfaltering Conviction to Pursue the Journey

A testament to the unfailing spirit, Dr. Nowlin's mission of bringing stewardship to all is one that offers hope to those who may be buried in darkness and needing a way to find the light. Any person who hopes to make a change would do well to read this book.

[ISBN 978-1-60266-068-7]

KIM LOGAN-NOWLIN AUTHOR, SPEAKER, TRAINER

Other Featured Books

The Attitude Adjustment of the Christian Man and Woman

Often, we become weary from the weight of the world and forget how to interact with those who love us. This book is so appropriate at a time when the world is in turmoil and more families are broken.

Through essays, scriptures, and parables filled with vital truths, the Nowlin's celebrate the power of God and our connections to Him. Practical techniques free us from pain and past disappointment and bring into us a new, fulfilling spirit, emotional and psychological stability, and sense of well-being.

[ISBN 1-594679-64-9]

KIM LOGAN-NOWLIN AUTHOR, SPEAKER, TRAINER

Other Featured Books

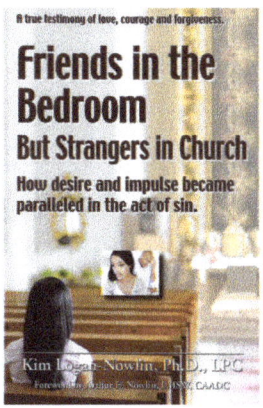

Friends in the Bedroom, But Strangers in Church

This book reveals a true dichotomy in the lifestyle of a young woman who was attacked by toxic desires. Although she attains maturity by way of a college degree, subsequent law school degree, and marrying her successful college sweetheart, she continues to fight compelling, consistent thoughts to enter dangerously into a relationship with her first attraction. When her fantasy becomes reality, her marriage and her faith are not strong enough to withstand her feelings, and she inevitably falls into deep sin.

Dr. Logan-Nowlin skillfully projected the insecurities and empowered this woman for over six years—therapeutically and spiritually—to take charge of the behaviors that consumed her. As her therapist, she helped the woman realize that inevitable consequences would eventually destroy her if she did not become proactive in the drastic decision to change her course in life.

[ISBN 978-1-4771-3864-9]

KIM LOGAN-NOWLIN AUTHOR, SPEAKER, TRAINER

Other Featured Books

Marriage: Living With the Unexplainable

"As you read the amazing stories in this book, I hope you will capture the true essence of Arthur and Kim Nowlin's intentions. They have drawn from real life experiences to share the amazing power of God in the realm of the impossible and the unexplainable as testified by the stories of individuals and couples traveling this freeway called life. This remarkable couple has joined together to form what I call the dynamic duo, championing the cause of God in the areas of marriage, family life, and mental health. I am sure your life will be positively impacted as you enjoy this latest undertaking, *Marriage: Living With the Unexplainable"* (*excerpt from foreword by Anthony J. Kelly, D.Min.*).

[ISBN 978-1-4984-1747-1]

KIM LOGAN-NOWLIN AUTHOR, SPEAKER, TRAINER

Other Featured Books

Intensive Care: Can My Marriage Survive or Not?

"The health of marriages has been under attack ever since the beginning when Adam and Eve's act of disobedience led to a series of arguments and passing of the blame that was only reconciled once the couple took personal accountability for their choices and surrendered everything to God—the architect of marriage. A threat to the health of one's marriage does not have to yield a terminal prognosis. It won't be easy, but it is possible to survive. This book will provide high quality care for couples who are currently on 'life support'" (*excerpt from foreword by Kenneth Anderson, M.S.*).

[ISBN 978-1-4984-7432-0]

Book Dr. Kim For Your Next Event

Kim Logan-Nowlin, Ph.D., LPC, BCPC, MFT, AAFLP or "Dr. Kim," as she is affectionately called by audiences, is a dynamic speaker who always leaves her audiences spellbound. For over 35 years, she has trained people from all walks of life to "Speak for Success." She holds a Bachelor of Science Degree in Special Education, Master of Arts Degree in Family and Guidance Counseling, and a Doctorate of Philosophy Degree in Oral and Interpersonal Communication and Clinical Family Counseling.

As a motivational speaker, her oratory brings encouragement, direction, hope, and healing to thousands each year as she travels around the U.S. and abroad sharing words of inspiration for all ages. She is a gifted woman on a mission to help others discover their gifts. Along with late husband and professional therapist Arthur Nowlin, they have met the needs of hurting individuals and families as Christian family counselors.

If you're looking for a powerful, energetic, passionate, influential, articulate, intelligent, motivational, and unforgettable presentation, you want Dr. Kim Logan-Nowlin.

If you need help making a more effective and bolder presentation for your company, or your organization needs new energy, Dr. Kim is the right person to excite and encourage your group to aim higher. She knows how to bring out the confidence and drive that so many of us possess but never use, and she gets results demonstrating the kinds of skills and leadership abilities necessary for success in whatever area you choose.

Live to Be Well conferences
Crisis Intervention conferences
Conflict Resolution conferences
Purity conferences
Marriage and Family retreats
Women's retreats
Men's retreats
Business retreats (Resolving Inner Communication Conflicts in the Workplace)
Leadership training (Mind over Matter)
Worship services
Teacher in-service programs
Special Spiritual events

Also providing training and development seminars, workshops and consulting on topics like:

Human Relations
Change Management: Paradigm Shift in Corporate America
Team Building
Workforce Diversity
Winning Leadership Strategies
Healthy Life-Style Management: Live to Be Well
*Customized courses and workshops available.

For booking or more information, contact:

Kim Logan-Nowlin, Ph.D., LPC, BCPC, MFT, ACAC, AFFLP

Kim Logan-Nowlin Communications, Inc.
3011 W. Grand Blvd. Suite 423
Detroit, Michigan 48202

(313) 664-4900
www.drkiminspires.com
drkimklc@gmail.com

About Kim Logan-Nowlin Communications Clinic, Inc.

Our Mission

Kim Logan-Nowlin Communications Clinic's mission is to offer education and treatment to the hearing and the hearing challenged in the areas of family and individual therapy; also, providing substance abuse treatment for alcohol and drugs.

Kim Logan-Nowlin Communications Clinic is committed to the community and offers support to individuals and families in need of positive lifestyle changes.

Kim Logan-Nowlin Communications Clinic emphasizes self-determination, self-worth, and self-evaluation toward altering negative experiences, and enhances opportunity for successful transition.

Kim Logan-Nowlin Communications Clinic will continue to serve the community through consistent support, and is committed to the concerns of individuals and families experiencing problems which prevent a healthy lifestyle.

Kim Logan-Nowlin Communications Clinic has been successfully addressing the needs of families and individuals experiencing problems, or those with marital concerns, by providing family therapy, child therapy, and substance abuse treatment.

Kim Logan-Nowlin Communications Clinic has provided employability training and substance abuse treatment to parole and probationary offenders since 1993.

About Kim Logan-Nowlin Communications Clinic, Inc..

Christian Family Counseling is committed to supporting individuals and families through the challenges of life.

Our staff of licensed professional therapists utilizes biblical principles to provide one-on-one and group counseling to people of all denominational backgrounds. Founder, Kim Logan-Nowlin has over 38 years of expertise in breaking the barriers of substance abuse, low self-esteem, and violence in order to build bridges to stronger relationships with God, improved communication, and reduce anxiety and stress.

Dr. Kim Logan-Nowlin's real life marriage and solid Christian foundation always provided strength to a generation facing crisis, degradation, and deterioration. Along with her late husband Arthur E. Nowlin LMSW, they co-hosted "Making

It Work" on the Dare to Dream 3ABN Christian Television Network, (2009-2016) a program that empowered countless families and restored many relationships. Their radio/cable television programs, "Speak for Success" and "Make It Last Forever" have revealed the concepts behind "Building Bridges and Breaking Barriers"—a dynamic philosophy intended to bridge the gaps, restructure the foundation and reestablish the roots in relationships.

Furthermore, Dr. Kim continues to conduct individual and group substance abuse sessions for ex-offenders under the Federal Bureau of Prisons, and she is a Certified HIV Counselor. From 2007-2014, the Nowlin's served as Family Life Directors of the Lake Region

Conference of the Seventh-day Adventist Church. Dr. Kim has been featured in *Essence Magazine, Message Magazine, Answers for Me* online publication, *Review and Herald, The Michigan Chronicle, The Michigan Front Page, Detroit Free Press,* and *Benton Harbor Spirit.* Dr. Kim has been the television host of "Live to Be Well" on the 3ABN Dare to Dream Christian Network since 2017. In June 2020, Dr. Kim joined www.36lccradio.com in Corpus Christi, Texas, as the host of the Live to Be Well Radio Talk Show. Dr. Kim's desire is to inspire everyone she meets to "Live to Be Well".

About Kim Logan-Nowlin Communications Clinic, Inc.

Our Services:
Group and Individual Counseling as well as workshops and lectures available in the following areas:

Adoption, Alcoholism, Anxiety, Bereavement Counseling, Child Abuse, Communication, Depression, Fear, Grief, Guilt, HIV Prevention, Marital Conflict, Parent-Child Issues, Phobias, Pre-Marital Counseling, Self-Esteem, Step-Parenting, Stress, Substance Abuse

We offer translation services for the hearing-challenged community.

Accreditation / Licenses:
American Psychological Association
Mental Health Professionals
Adventist Association of Family Life Professionals
Licensed by the Federal Bureau of Prisons

State of Michigan Licensed Professional Counselor
Board Certified Professional Counselor
Certified HIV Counselor
American Psychotherapy Association Diplomat

"Don't let your beginning be your end."
Dr. Kim Logan-Nowlin

CPSIA information can be obtained
at www.ICGtesting.com
Printed in the USA
LVHW070400040621
689240LV00009B/237